Wheels Around Cork

by
Cyril McIntyre

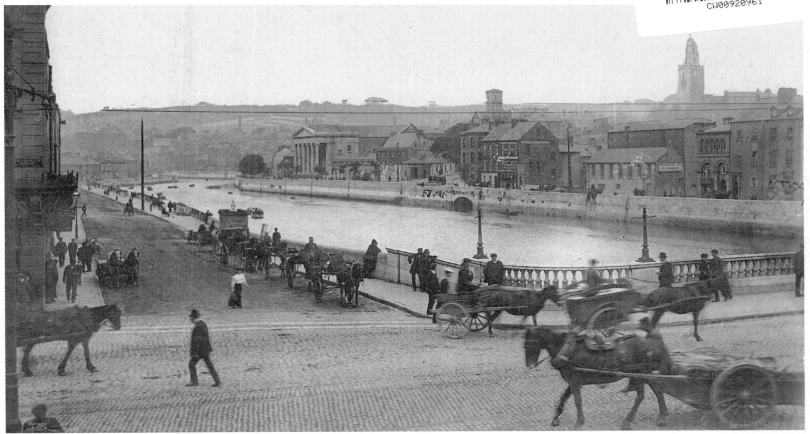

A view of St Patrick's Bridge showing a variety of forms of horse-drawn transport: open carts, a delivery float and traditional sidecars. In the background, on Pope's Quay, is the Dominican Church of St Mary with its distinctive Ionic portico. Overlooking the tranquil scene is the Shandon Church of St Ann, built in 1722 and known worldwide as a symbol of Cork. It has been immortalised by the poet Francis Sylvester Mahony, better known as 'Father Prout', whose best-known work tells of 'the bells of Shandon, that sound so grand on the pleasant waters of the River Lee'.

ISBN 1 84033 247 6

The publishers regret that they cannot supply
copies of any pictures featured in this book.

PATRICK STREET AND BRIDGE, CORK.

R.203

A typical postcard view of St Patrick's Bridge and the Statue dating from the mid-1930s. The low levels of car ownership in those far-off days is indicated by the absence of much traffic other than the Leyland buses of the Great Southern Railways Omnibus Department.

FOREWORD

Both the city and county of Cork have always had a rich heritage, not only in literary and historical terms but also in the variety of their transport systems over many years. With its deep water port, the city became a natural focus of road and rail networks, while the transatlantic liner terminal at Cobh, at the mouth of Cork harbour, saw many thousands of both emigrants and tourists over several generations. At one time during the latter part of the nineteenth century Cork could boast of no less than six railway termini, two of which were once linked by a short-lived horse tramway. When electric trams arrived on the scene, the track was built to a unique gauge of two feet eleven and a half inches so as to provide a link between two narrow-gauge railways. After the disappearance of the trams in 1931, double-deck buses became a feature of Cork's transport six years before such vehicles commenced operating regular services in Dublin.

My selection of photographs is very much a personal memoir. It traces the origins of Cork's varied forms of wheeled transport from the mid-nineteenth century onwards and also reflects the middle years of the twentieth century, when 'I sported and played, 'neath each green leafy shade, on the banks of my own lovely Lee'. In the case of photographs other than my own, I have sought permission for publication and credited the original photographer where he or she is known. However, a number of photographs in my collection are anonymous and thus I have been unable to credit the source. Some of these are old picture postcards, while others have been handed down from former bus companies or vehicle manufacturers which have long since passed into history.

The Cork Omnibus Company, owned by Smyth of Princes' Street, was a user of Guy buses. As well as the traditional 20-seater (shown here) and 26-seater types, the company also owned a forward-control 32-seater immortalised in a local ballad as 'the big COC'. Smyth operated mainly on the Blackrock route, using five buses to maintain a ten minute frequency. The Cork Omnibus Company ceased operations sometime during 1932.

The coming of the railways in the second half of the nineteenth century opened up many parts of Cork and Kerry to tourist traffic for the first time. Horse-drawn touring cars took the pioneering tourists to the more remote areas which the railways did not reach. At Gougane Barra, source of the River Lee and site of a monastic settlement founded by St Finbarr in the seventh century, Cronin's Hotel was a popular intermediate stop on what was advertised from 1898 as 'The Tourist's Route'. The tourists travelled by rail from Cork to Macroom, continuing by road to Killarney through Inchigeela, Gougane Barra and Glengarriff. These cars were drawn by three or four horses and carried up to fourteen passengers. *(National Library of Ireland)*

Crosshaven, about fifteen miles from the city, has been a favourite seaside resort for generations of Corkonians. From 1850 to 1900 trains from Cork ran as far as Passage West, where a fleet of small steamers provided connections to other parts of Cork harbour, including Crosshaven. From there, travel to the many coves and inlets favoured by holidaymakers from the city was by horse-drawn wagonette; this one is designated for 'Church Bay and Waver's Point'. After the Cork, Blackrock & Passage Railway was extended to Crosshaven in 1904 the wagonettes connected with the trains. Harbour excursions continued to be popular right up to the 1950s. *(National Library of Ireland)*

The oldest of the tourist routes in Munster was the 'Prince of Wales' Route' which had been followed by King Edward VII when, as Prince of Wales, he visited Ireland in 1858. The basic route was from Cork to Bantry, initially by road and later by rail, continuing to Glengarriff either by steamer or mail car. From Glengarriff the journey was by mail car to Kenmare and onwards to Killarney. In later years a company called Tourist Development (Ireland) Limited operated horse coach services in conjunction with the railway, offering daily services during the summer season at inclusive ticket rates. By 1910 the horses had given way to a fleet of Commer fourteen-seat charabancs, one of which is seen here at Glengarriff.

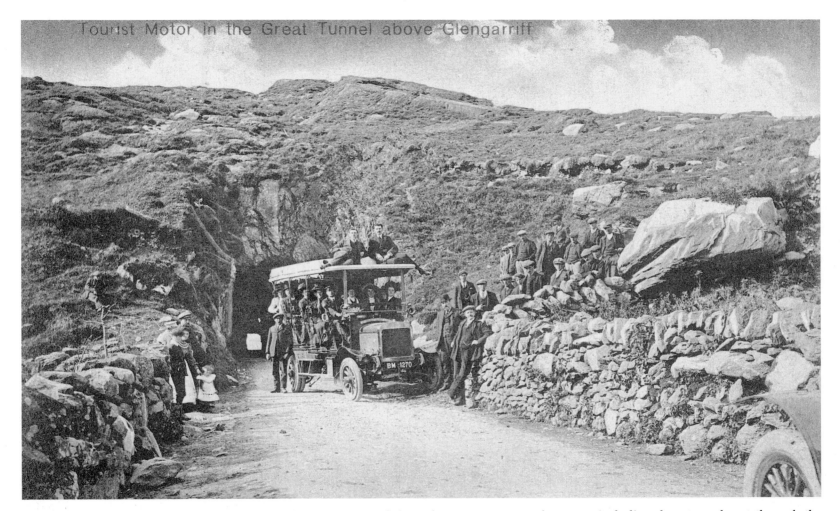

Between Glengarriff and Kenmare the touring charabancs passed through some very rugged scenery, including three tunnels cut through the mountainside. This was a favourite location for photographers gathering material to illustrate guidebooks and producing picture postcards. Both this view, and that at Glengarriff featured opposite, were published as postcards by Fergus O'Connor of Dublin, although printed in Germany. In all up to twenty charabancs were used on the Tourist Development Company routes; most of them were registered in Bedfordshire by Commer Cars of Luton before delivery to Ireland. The outbreak of war in 1914 put an end to the programme of touring services and most of the charabancs found further use in other parts of Ireland.

One of the vessels owned by the Cork, Blackrock & Passage Railway was the paddle steamer *Albert*, seen here departing from St Patrick's Quay on a Sunday afternoon packed to capacity with excursionists. The bridge, lifted for the departure, carried the Cork City Railway which from 1912 to 1976 provided a link between the 'Dublin station' at Lower Glanmire Road and the 'Bandon station' at Albert Quay (to the right of where the photographer stood). A coal boat occupies the berth outside the offices of the Clyde Shipping Company. Rising in the background are the slopes of Montenotte, site of many elegant Georgian and Victorian houses with fine views of the city and the port. The *Albert* was built in 1882 and remained on the Lee until 1925. (*National Library of Ireland*)

In 1901 the village of Douglas, three miles from the city, still retained its rural character and both trams and photographers were enough of a novelty to attract adults as well as children willing to pose for the camera. Tram No. 26 displays the letters 'D S' indicating the route as Douglas to the Statue. The primitive road surface is evident and the track is almost covered with mud. The postcard caption described Douglas as 'a very pretty village, connected with Cork by electric tram, the run taking about half an hour, with two tweed factories whose products have a reputation through the world'.

Cork came into the electric tramway era when the Cork Electric Tramways & Lighting Company ran its first trams on 22 December 1898. It was a narrow-gauge tramway, built to a gauge a half-inch less than the Irish rail narrow gauge of three feet. It was intended to run trains through the city streets from the Cork & Muskerry Railway to the Cork, Blackrock & Passage Railway; the half-inch reduction was necessary to allow the tapered railway wheel flanges to use the tramway rail, but the through running never materialised. One of the tramway's six terminal points was at St Luke's Cross on Summerhill, illustrated here. The tram is just ready to leave for Sunday's Well at the other end of the line. In the background is the imposing Church of Ireland parish church of St Luke. The kiosk in the centre of the junction to the right was a former toll booth.

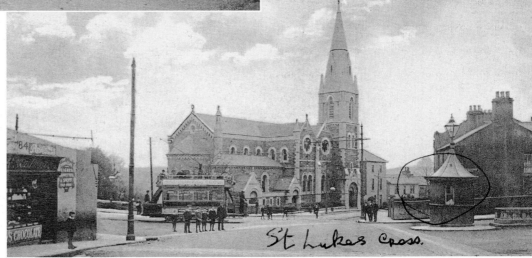

St Lukes Cross.

Western Road, Cork.

For about a mile along the Western Road in Cork the tramway line and the track of the Cork & Muskerry Railway ran alongside each other. At certain times of the day the bizarre sight of a tram and train appearing to 'race' each other could be seen. The Muskerry line opened from Cork to Blarney on 8 August 1887. A branch to Coachford opened on 18 March 1888 and another branch to Donoughmore opened on 6 May 1893. The entire Muskerry system closed on 30 December 1934.

Mardyke Walk, Cork.

M. 223.

The Mardyke Walk is a mile-long promenade running between the north and south channels of the River Lee and shaded by elm trees. It is as popular a walk today as it was in Victorian times, when only the occasional child's tricycle or private carriage would disturb the thoughts of leisurely strollers.

11

Grand Parade, Cork.

M. 223.

This view of the Grand Parade, the widest street in Cork, dates from the mid-1920s. A few cars and a solitary truck give little indication of the huge volumes of motor traffic of later years, while one or two early buses are just visible in the background. Tram No. 4 en route to Sunday's Well prepares to turn right into Washington Street. The road junction here became known to generations of Cork people as Singer's Corner, from the Singer sewing machine shop which remains a familiar landmark to this day.

Cork's central landmark is the Father Mathew Statue at the north end of Patrick Street, erected in 1864 as a memorial to Father Theobald Mathew who founded the temperance movement in Ireland. Known simply as 'the Statue' to Cork people the world over, it was the hub of the tramway system and plays a similar role in the extended network of city bus routes today. The eventual shape of the tramway system, from about 1902 onwards, was three cross-city routes: Blackpool to Douglas, Summerhill to Sunday's Well and Tivoli to Blackrock. The absence of traffic in this view of Tram No. 19 on the northbound track suggests that it was taken on a Sunday morning. (*National Library of Ireland*)

One of the earliest operators of motor charabancs in Cork was the Cork & Ballycotton Motor Service Company. Their passenger transport venture was short-lived, but they remain today as motor dealers, trading as the CAB Motor Co. This Dennis charabanc, registered in Waterford, was photographed at the South Mall, possibly on its first outing. The date has been suggested as May 1912, the occasion of a trip by the old Nils football team to play a match somewhere in mid-Cork. The man seated at the back of the vehicle, just in front of the canvas hood, bears a striking resemblance to Terence MacSwiney, later elected Lord Mayor of Cork, who died on hunger strike in 1920 during the War of Independence. The Irish tricolour flag is visible outside the Norwich Union office.

St. Patrick Street, Cork.

M. 223.

The growth of motor traffic is very much in evidence in this view of Patrick Street dating from the summer of 1926. In June of that year Captain A. P. Morgan, a London bus proprietor, started the Cork Motor Services using five Daimler open-top double deckers imported from London. Two routes were operated – from College Road to Sunday's Well and from the Statue to Collins Barracks. Here one of the Daimlers (MF 9241) passes Roche's Stores en route to College Road, preceded by a tram bound for Douglas and an unidentified single decker bus.

Another view of Patrick Street, with tram No. 8 showing the destination 'Douglas' and No. 24 showing 'Blackrock' despite being on the northbound track. Between the two trams is the tramway maintenance car used to spray water between the tracks to keep down the dust. Another of the Cork Motor Services' double deckers is bound for College Road, while St Patrick's Bridge and Hill stretch away into the background. Captain Morgan's venture did not last long; by September services had ceased and the buses had been sent back to London. However, other local bus owners expanded their services and succeeded in taking a lot of tramway passengers over the following few years.

The first bus services into Cork from towns in the county started on 13 October 1926, when Southern Motorways commenced running between Fermoy and Cork. This company, owned by the Swanton family of Cobh, later expanded its operations to include routes to Cobh, Bandon, Macroom and Blarney, before selling the business to the Irish Omnibus Company in January 1930. As well as Reo and Vulcan buses, they also operated a solitary Mercedes–Benz (PI 4290) with bodywork by O'Gorman Brothers of Clonmel. It was photographed on the Bandon service, outside the Cork terminus and office at the Methodist Central Hall in Academy Street.

Another pioneering local bus operator in Cork was Jeremiah Dwyer, based at Rocksavage near the Albert Quay railway terminus. He traded at various times as the Magnet, Rocksavage Omnibus Company (ROC) and the Leeside Motor Service. His principal routes were to Crosshaven and Monkstown in competition with the Cork, Blackrock & Passage Railway, and also to Kinsale. For a time he also ran a service between the Statue and Blackrock which competed with the trams, but was later refused a licence for this route by the City Commissioner. This Guy 26-seater on the Crosshaven route in 1930 is typical of the Dwyer fleet, which was acquired by the Irish Omnibus Company in March 1932.

December 1930. Trams bound for Blackrock and Sunday's Well are followed across St Patrick's Bridge into Patrick Street by a Leyland Lion single decker of the Irish Omnibus Company. The IOC had by this time become the major provider of bus services in Cork city and county. Going about their Christmas shopping amid the decorated streets, few people realised that this would be the last Christmas of the trams. Following the inauguration of the Shannon hydroelectric scheme, takeover of the electric supply part of the business by the new Electricity Supply Board was inevitable. This was soon followed by the announcement, from the company's head office in London, that the tramway system would close at the end of March 1931.

The Irish Sleeper Omnibus Service, run by Furey's Tours of Dublin, quickly became the centre of attraction outside the Victoria Hotel in Patrick Street when it arrived on its inaugural trip in January 1929. The Associated Daimler chassis was fitted with Strachan coachwork, designed to accommodate 32 seated passengers in day service or sixteen passengers in sleeping berths for overnight service. The coach was also fitted with a toilet and buffet and was painted blue, white and mauve. The service ran on alternate nights in each direction, but unfortunately did not prove a viable commercial venture and ceased operation after only a few weeks. The coach was then used on tours and special trips and was later rebuilt to normal layout after a fire completely gutted its interior at Clane in County Kildare.

A quiet Sunday afternoon sees tram No. 19 trundling along the South Mall from Douglas, about to pass a solitary parked bus and a few outside cars, or 'jingles', further along the street. The spires of St Finbarre's Church of Ireland Cathedral can just be seen in the distant background; the cathedral was designed by William Burgess in the French Early Pointed style and consecrated in 1870. (*Irish Tourist Association*)

Another of the many popular views of Patrick Street near the Statue, with the ubiquitous water wagon parked in front of the famous 'Statue Hut' used by the tramway inspectors as an office. Tram No. 34 heads for Sunday's Well, while an IOC single decker (Associated Daimler ZI 1788) proclaims its destination as 'Douglas'. Taxis stand along the centre of the street alongside the tram tracks and early signs of parking congestion are evident beside the crowded footpath outside Roche's Stores. (*Irish Tourist Association*)

On what was planned to be the final day of tramway operation – Tuesday 31 March 1931 – tram No. 17 loads for Summerhill at the Statue in torrential rain, with a tram for Blackpool last in the line of three cars. Unusually for this period there are no buses to be seen. In the event, the IOC bus fleet proved inadequate to meet the demands of the travelling public after withdrawal of the trams. Following pressure from Cork Corporation and local Dáil deputies, including President Cosgrave, the IOC agreed to work the trams for six months until new buses were delivered to augment the city fleet. Seven days later, on Tuesday 7 April, the trams returned to the streets and continued to work the familiar routes until the 'real' closure on 30 September.

Some of the new buses for Cork pictured at Broadstone depot in Dublin before their delivery in September 1931. The additional fleet comprised twelve Leyland Lion 32-seater single deckers and six Leyland Titan 51-seater double deckers. The double deckers were imported complete with Leyland bodies, while the single deckers were bodied by the Great Southern Railways at Inchicore works using Leyland drawings.

Crossing St Patrick's Bridge en route to Dillon's Cross, IOC double decker No. 802 displays the Guinness advertising which was to be a feature of all double deckers in Cork for almost 40 years. This campaign of Guinness advertising may have been influenced by the presence in Cork of two long-established local breweries – Beamish & Crawford and Murphy's. Cork people always had a strong loyalty to their local brands and were not easily persuaded to change their drinking preferences in favour of what were perceived as 'foreign' products! (© Alan B. Cross – from W. Noel Jackson Collection)

The first day of October 1931 saw Father Mathew look down on a street scene again bereft of trams, but this time they were gone for good. The Statue Hut was taken over by the IOC bus inspector and continued to be the focal point of bus services in the city until its removal in 2002 as part of an urban renewal scheme for Patrick Street. Here an older Leyland Lion bus works the Douglas–Blackpool route, while one of the double deckers is destined for Dillon's Cross, on the extension of the tramway route beyond Summerhill. One of the new Leyland Lion buses waits at the back.

It was not only the electric trams which suffered the effects of competing motor traffic in the lean economic conditions of the 1930s. The Great Southern Railways had come under severe pressure since its formation in 1925 and narrow gauge lines were an early target for closure. The two Cork lines – the Muskerry and the Passage – which had once hoped to link up using the tramway system were soon to be consigned to history. At Albert Street station, locomotive No. 7 – a 2-4-2T built in 1900 by Neilson's – is ready to depart with a Crosshaven train. The section of the Passage line from Monkstown to Crosshaven was closed on 31 May 1932, followed by the section from Monkstown to Cork on 10 September. The Muskerry line closed on 30 December 1934.

Working the Cork to Ballingeary route in 1932, Leyland Lion No. 330 (ZI 881) of the Irish Omnibus Company pauses outside William's Hotel in Macroom. Canvas awnings to protect shop window displays from sunlight were a common feature of many business premises, as were roadside petrol pumps and oil cabinets. At this stage many bus company staff were still not supplied with any uniform other than a cap and sometimes a dustcoat, although in later years a full uniform became the norm.

At Macroom on a summer's day in 1939, before the clouds of war had gathered, the GSR service from Killarney to Cork waits for passengers. The bus (No. 912, PI 8542) is a Leyland Lion with 32-seater body built at the GSR Inchicore works. This was the standard type of country bus built by the GSR between 1934 and 1940; many continued to be a familiar sight in Cork city and county well into the 1950s.

Just as it was in the days of horse-drawn touring cars (see page 4), Cronin's Hotel in Gougane Barra continued to be a popular stop for bus tours. Transport photography was not widely practiced as a hobby in the 1930s, but at least one member of the party is keen to improve his photograph of the GSR Leyland Tiger bus by standing on a chair!

A Morris-Commercial truck owned by a local co-operative creamery wends its way across Youghal Bridge with a cargo of milk churns. The crude barriers of tar barrels and planks were erected to ensure that drivers had no option but to comply with the speed limit of five miles per hour. It was to be January 1963 before a new bridge was completed and opened for traffic. *(CIE)*

The Marina works of the Ford Motor Company was the biggest employer in Cork for many years. The famous Model T car was built there, as well as thousands of Fordson tractors for export all over Europe. From 1932 onwards it became an assembly plant, assembling a range of Ford cars and goods vehicles for the Irish market. With a carrying capacity of four tons, the Ford Surrey six-wheel truck was in widespread use throughout Ireland. It was the standard medium-weight truck of the Great Southern Railways' road freight department which had almost 300 Surreys in the fleet. This example dates from 1935. *(CIE)*

In October 1944 the terminal for country buses was moved from Grand Parade to Parnell Place. A few months later, on 1 January 1945, the Great Southern Railways amalgamated with the Dublin United Transport Company to create a new national transport organisation – Córas Iompair Éireann. This view of the bus terminal in July 1946 shows three Leyland Tiger buses of the former GSR fleet in the CIE livery of olive green and eau-de-nil. The author's mother waits to board the Raffeen bus; beside her is his father, in inspector's uniform. *(John C. Gillham)*

During the summer of 1947 Cork received its first delivery of new buses since 1940. This batch of fifteen Leyland Tiger single deckers had an unusual history. The chassis were delivered to the GSR in 1941 but remained unassembled throughout the war years because of a shortage of body parts. They were completed by CIE as 35-seat buses but because they lacked the traditional roof luggage carrier they were of limited use on rural routes and were later transferred to city services in both Cork and Limerick. Here, on a busy day on the Killarney to Cork route, T 22, one of the buses delivered in 1947, is pictured (centre) behind TP 70 (formerly GSR 244) at the usual stop in the Main Street of Macroom. *(The Omnibus Society – John F. Parke Collection)*

Delays in obtaining new buses in the aftermath of World War II led to many pre-war vehicles remaining in service for far longer than had been planned when they were first bought. This Leyland Titan double decker (R 249, formerly GSR 822) was built in 1936 and remained in service on city routes in Cork until 1956. The bus at the back of this line-up near the Statue is from a batch of ten double deckers bought by the GSR in 1940. *(R. F. Mack)*

On a clear day in 1949, Leyland Tiger TF 11 (formerly GSR 794) en route from Cork to Ringaskiddy waits opposite the former railway station at Monkstown. In the background beside the River Lee is the former railway trackbed, by now converted to a pedestrian walkway. The children on the footpath are the author and his sister.

On the evening of Tuesday 7 December 1948 there was torrential rain and flooding throughout County Cork. Near Mourne Abbey, between Cork and Mallow on the main road to Limerick, a bridge known locally as Hackett's Bridge was washed away by flood waters. Buses had to terminate at either side of the bridge and passengers walked across on a remaining section of roadway about four feet wide. A temporary bridge was erected by army engineers from Collins Barracks in Cork and this remained in use for several months while the road was realigned and a new bridge constructed. The first bus across the temporary bridge was Leyland Tiger T 1 (formerly GSR 463), built in 1934 and one of the small number of diesel-engined buses operated by the Great Southern Railways. (CIE)

Locomotive No. 36 of the former Great Southern & Western Railway has been on display at the railway station on Lower Glanmire Road for many years. Built in 1845 by Bury Curtis & Kennedy of Liverpool, it is reputed to have hauled the first train to run from Dublin to Cork in October 1849 and worked trains on the line until 1874. During that time it covered about half a million miles and frequently achieved speeds of up to 60 miles per hour.

The most powerful railway locomotives ever to run in Ireland were the Queen class of the Great Southern Railways, built in 1939 for the express passenger and mail trains on the Dublin to Cork route. Numbered 800–802 they were named *Maedhbh*, *Macha* and *Táilte* after queens featuring in Celtic legend. This is the only known photograph of all three Queen class locomotives together, and was taken at the locomotive yard in Cork on 16 September 1949. The occasion was the operation of two special trains carrying the Boston Archdiocesan Pilgrimage from Cork to Dublin, after their arrival at Cobh by transatlantic liner. Locomotives 800 and 801, specially decorated with Irish and papal flags, hauled the two pilgrimage specials, while 802 worked the scheduled 12.30 p.m. service from Cork on the same day. Locomotive 800, *Maedhbh*, is now preserved in the Ulster Folk and Transport Museum at Cultra near Belfast. *(CIE)*

A feature of CIE road freight operations for many years was a network of overnight express routes for delivery of the national newspapers from Dublin to various parts of the country. The service to Cork departed Dublin every night at 2 a.m. and with a number of intermediate stops was scheduled to arrive in Cork at 7.30 a.m. Speed and reliability were essential to ensure that the news got through and in 1948 the first vehicles in a fleet of over 100 new Leyland Comet lorries were allocated to this work. On an early summer's morning, after some overnight showers, Comet ZH 4028 heads for an on-time arrival into Cork. *(CIE)*

A later generation of Leyland Comet lorries for express newspaper deliveries is represented by L 101, seen at Capwell Garage in 1957. By way of variation, these trucks were painted in the reversed two-tone green colour scheme used on CIE tour coaches. As was the case with most CIE vehicles up to the advent of European free trade, the chassis were imported in kit form for assembly at the Broadstone works in Dublin, while the cabs were of a CIE design emanating from the Spa Road bodybuilding plant.

Throughout the period of operation of transatlantic liner services to and from Cobh there were also occasional visits by cruise liners to Bantry Bay. Passengers came ashore at Glengarriff and availed themselves of local coach tours operated by CIE. Here a shore excursion pauses at one of the many scenic vantage points on the Prince of Wales' Route. Built in 1954, the luxurious Leyland Royal Tiger coaches were of a very futuristic design and had the engine mounted under the floor in the centre of the chassis. Painted in a new colour scheme of primrose yellow and grey, they were individually named after Irish rivers. *(CIE)*

Every Thursday for many years saw the arrival in Cork at 11.15 a.m. of the bus from Castletownbere, a journey of 93 miles which took just over four hours. It terminated at the West Cork pub in Parnell Place, opposite the CIE bus station. Run by O'Donoghue's of The Corner House in Castletownbere, and still serving the people of the Beara peninsula today, this is the sole survivor of the many independent bus services which ran to Cork from the 1920s onwards. The blue and cream Bedford coach dated from 1954 and was originally operated by James Culloty of Killarney on tours of the Ring of Kerry. It was bought by the Berehaven Bus Service in 1957. The bus departed again at 5 30 p.m. on Thursday evenings.

Another local bus operator in Cork during the 1950s was Donal Canny of Anglesea Street. He concentrated on private hire excursion work and also ran special services to dances and sporting events. In 1959 he started a service from Cork to carry workers engaged on the construction of the oil refinery at Whitegate. One of the additional buses obtained for the work was this Albion Valkyrie 35-seater, built in 1938 with bodywork by Harkness Coachworks of Belfast. Originally operated by the Major Bus Service of Belfast, it passed through three other bus fleets before ending its days in Cork.

For many years the standard country bus in the CIE fleet was the Leyland Tiger with 39-seat bodywork built at the Spa Road works in Dublin. The sunken roof luggage carrier, reached by a ladder at the back, was an essential feature for carriage of parcels, luggage and bicycles. P 33 was photographed in July 1960 near Albert Quay railway station, which from January 1959 to October 1960 also provided temporary terminal facilities for buses during the construction of a new bus station on the Parnell Place site. This bus was built in 1948 and remained in service until 1964, including a period on hire to the County Donegal Railways Joint Committee.

A Leyland Tiger bus dating from 1938, formerly GSR 248, ends its days rather ingloriously after use as a temporary office in the City car park, off the Grand Parade, in August 1957. The asking price was £50 – a trifling sum by today's standards, but at the time the equivalent of three months' wages for a junior clerk in the Parnell Place bus office!

The Cork City Railway link line, between the stations at Lower Glanmire Road and Albert Quay, saw in its heyday of operations up to twenty trains of freight wagons each weekday. Invariably these trains were worked by locomotive 217, of 0-6-0 tank design. Each train on this line had to be preceded by a flagman with a red flag and the fireman also had to ring a large bell frequently throughout the journey.

Like Lower Glanmire Road station (see page 35), Mallow railway station had its own historical display for a number of years. Locomotive No. 90 was originally built for the Fermoy and Mitchelstown branch and later worked between Timoleague and Courtmacsherry on the West Cork system. A combination of light track and sharp curves on the Courtmacsherry line required the use of light locomotives. The entire West Cork railway network closed in March 1961.

This busy scene at the Statue provides evidence of the explosion in levels of car ownership through the early 1960s. By this time the pre-war double deckers had all gone, to be replaced by Leyland Titan 66-seater vehicles such as the one in the foreground which became the standard CIE city bus of the period. En route to the developing northside suburb of Ballyvolane, R 699, painted in a new blue and cream livery, is flanked by a P type single decker in red and cream bound for Spangle Hill (since renamed Farranree). Bicycles and motor scooters jostle for the best starting position as they await the signal to proceed from the Garda on point duty at St Patrick's Bridge.

In 1978 CIE introduced a summer seasonal Expressway coach service taking in the traditional Prince of Wales' Route from Cork to Killarney. This Leyland Leopard (M 190) was photographed at Glengarriff en route to Kenmare and Killarney on a pre-launch publicity trip. Built in 1972, it was painted in the CIE Expressway livery of signal red and traffic yellow. *(CIE)*

After closure of the Cork City Railway link line in 1976, the railway tracks on Brian Boru Bridge and Clontarf Bridge remained in place for another three years, as did the bridge lifting gear and associated control cabins. In 1979 the tracks were finally lifted and the redundant superstructure removed. Here a coach on hire to Olson Tours crosses Brian Boru Bridge after it reopened to traffic on 3 June 1980. *(J. St Leger)*

Opened in October 1960, the new bus station building at Parnell Place offered bus passengers a vast improvement in facilities over the old premises which had been in use since 1944. It quickly became a city landmark and benefited later from redevelopment of the quayside area between Parnell Place and St Patrick's Bridge. By the beginning of the twenty-first century local and long-distance bus traffic had outgrown the original facilities, at which point Bus Éireann, as successor to CIE, refurbished and extended the station. *(CIE)*